THE CIVIL WAR

THE FORMATION OF THE CONFEDERACY

by Russell Roberts

FOCUS
READERS

VOYAGER

www.focusreaders.com

Focus Readers is distributed by North Star Editions:
sales@northstareditions.com | 888-417-0195

Produced for Focus Readers by Red Line Editorial.

Content Consultant: Dr. Gideon Mailer, Associate Professor of History, University of Minnesota Duluth

Photographs ©: Library of Congress, cover, 1; E. & H. T. Anthony/Brady's National Photographic Portrait Galleries/Emily Howland Photograph Album/Library of Congress, 4–5; Tong_stocker/Shutterstock Images, 7; J. H. Lakin/Library of Congress, 8–9; Frederick De Bourg Richards/Marian S. Carson Collection/Library of Congress, 11; McPherson & Oliver/Liljenquist Family Collection of Civil War Photographs/Library of Congress, 13; Liljenquist Family Collection of Civil War Photographs/Library of Congress, 15, 20; Brady-Handy Photograph Collection/Library of Congress, 16–17; Red Line Editorial, 18, 31, 41; Everett Historical/Shutterstock Images, 22–23, 38–39, 42; Glasshouse Images/Newscom, 25; Selden J. Woodman/Cooper & Co./Library of Congress, 26; William Shaw/Library of Congress, 28–29; AP Images, 32–33; Mathew B. Brady/Library of Congress, 35; Mccallk69/Shutterstock Images, 36; Fotosearch/Archive Photos/Getty Images, 45

Library of Congress Cataloging-in-Publication Data
Names: Roberts, Russell, 1953- author.
Title: The formation of the Confederacy / Russell Roberts.
Description: Lake Elmo : Focus Readers, 2020. | Series: The civil war |
  Includes bibliographical references and index. | Audience: Grades 7-9
Identifiers: LCCN 2019036400 (print) | LCCN 2019036401 (ebook) | ISBN
  9781644930816 (hardcover) | ISBN 9781644931608 (paperback) | ISBN
  9781644933183 (pdf) | ISBN 9781644932391 (ebook)
Subjects: LCSH: United States--History--Civil War,
  1861-1865--Causes--Juvenile literature. | Confederate States of
  America--History--Juvenile literature. | Secession--Southern
  States--Juvenile literature. | Southern States--Politics and
  government--1775-1865--Juvenile literature. | United States--Politics
  and government--1815-1861--Juvenile literature.
Classification: LCC E459 .R576 2020 (print) | LCC E459 (ebook) | DDC
  973.7/11--dc23
LC record available at https://lccn.loc.gov/2019036400
LC ebook record available at https://lccn.loc.gov/2019036401

Printed in the United States of America
Mankato, MN
012020

ABOUT THE AUTHOR

Russell Roberts is an award-winning freelance writer who has written and published more than 75 books for both children and adults. Among his children's books are biographies, examinations of famous buildings, and stories about characters from Greek mythology.

TABLE OF CONTENTS

CHAPTER 1

A VICIOUS ATTACK

In early 1856, the mood in the US Senate was tense. Several areas of land had been added to the United States. Southern lawmakers wanted these areas to allow slavery. Many Northern lawmakers did not. Debates dragged on for weeks.

Then, on May 22, the conflict turned physical. South Carolina representative Preston Brooks entered the Senate. He strode to the desk where Massachusetts senator Charles Sumner sat.

Senator Charles Sumner was an outspoken opponent of slavery.

Before Sumner had a chance to stand, Brooks struck him on the head with a cane. Sumner fell forward. His legs were caught under the desk, so he could not escape. He lay trapped as Brooks hit him again and again. Brooks struck more than 30 times before his cane broke into pieces.

Sumner was badly hurt. The attack outraged Northerners. But many Southerners were proud of Brooks. Some people even bought him new canes. One thing was clear. The United States was a deeply divided country.

The North and the South had developed differently during the first half of the 1800s. The South contained mostly small towns and villages. Its economy was based on agriculture. The region grew cotton, tobacco, and other crops. Its large farms and plantations depended on the labor of enslaved workers.

△ Tobacco was the main crop grown in North Carolina.

In contrast, the North focused more on manufacturing. Large cities such as New York and Boston dotted the region. As immigrants came to the United States, the populations of these cities soared. As the cities grew, so did the factories.

By 1804, slavery was illegal in most Northern states. Some Northern lawmakers wanted to ban slavery in any new **territories** and states as well. Lawmakers from the South saw this idea as a major threat. The tension led to several political battles throughout the 1800s. Most of them focused on the expansion of slavery.

CHAPTER 2

POLITICAL PROBLEMS

As the United States grew, so did the conflict about slavery. In 1817, Missouri applied to join the Union as a slave state. Southerners wanted to bring enslaved people there to plant cotton and other crops. But many Northerners didn't want any more states to allow slavery.

At the time, there were 11 slave states and 11 free states. Keeping this balance was important. Each state had two lawmakers in the US Senate.

Many enslaved workers endured long days of forced labor in cotton fields.

If another slave state joined, there would be more proslavery senators. They could pass laws supporting their views.

In February 1819, a Northern lawmaker proposed banning slavery in Missouri. Southern lawmakers opposed him. The two sides argued for weeks. One lawmaker spoke for four straight days. Finally, they agreed to compromise. Missouri would be a slave state. But Maine would become a free state to keep the balance. In addition, the country would be divided at the 36°30′ parallel. This latitude line runs across the United States. Slavery would be illegal in new territories to the north of it. Areas to the south would allow slavery.

The Missouri Compromise ended one conflict. But another soon arose. In 1828, Congress passed a **tariff** law. It protected industry in Northern states. Southern states protested. They called it

△ Senator Henry Clay helped create several compromises during the 1800s.

illegal and unfair. When Congress passed a similar law in 1832, South Carolina refused to pay either tax. Its leaders said the laws went against the state's rights. They even threatened to **secede**.

Congress suggested using the military to enforce the laws. Congress also lowered the tax. As a result, South Carolina agreed to remain in the Union. A tentative balance between free states and slave states continued.

After the Mexican–American War (1846–1848), the United States gained a huge area of land in the West. Northern lawmakers suggested banning slavery there. In response, some Southern states considered seceding.

Once again, Congress planned a compromise. California would become a free state. Buying and selling enslaved people would become illegal in Washington, DC, though slavery would still be allowed. And in the rest of the land from Mexico, slavery would not be forbidden by Congress.

The Compromise of 1850 also toughened the **Fugitive** Slave Act. This **federal** law required all states to send escaped slaves back to slaveholders. Many Northerners had chosen not to. But the updated law said federal officials could force people to return fugitives. Any suspected runaways could be arrested, even in free states.

These two men escaped slavery in the 1800s.

Professional slave hunters rushed to Northern cities. Some captured people who had been living freely in the North for years. Thousands of black Americans fled to Canada. Many Northerners were furious. A few even attacked people who were taking supposed runaways back to the South.

HARRIET BEECHER STOWE

The updated Fugitive Slave Act faced some opposition in the North. **Abolitionists** wrote and spoke against it. Harriet Beecher Stowe was one of them. "Such peril and shame as now hangs over this country is worse than Roman slavery," she wrote in 1851. "I hope every woman who can write will not be silent."[1]

Taking her own advice, Stowe wrote a novel by candlelight in her kitchen. She called it *Uncle Tom's Cabin*. The book presented slavery as evil and brutal. Stowe explained that she wrote it because "as a woman, as a mother, I was oppressed and brokenhearted with the sorrows and injustice I saw."[2]

The novel was published in 1852. It sold 300,000 copies in just one year. Many people

△ During the 1800s, Harriet Beecher Stowe's novel sold more copies than every book except the Bible.

in the North who had not thought much about slavery began to oppose it after they read *Uncle Tom's Cabin*. Stowe's writing made readers feel sympathy for enslaved people.

In contrast, many Southerners hated Stowe's novel. These readers often supported slavery. As a result, they saw the book as an attack on their way of life. In some places, *Uncle Tom's Cabin* was outlawed. Even so, many people in Southern states read and bought it.

1. Joan D. Hendrick. *Harriet Beecher Stowe: A Life*. New York: Oxford University Press, 1994. 208.
2. Hendrick. *Harriet Beecher Stowe*. 237.

CHAPTER 3

KANSAS BLEEDS

For a few years, the Compromise of 1850 seemed to be working. Many people believed that the crisis had passed and the Union was safe. But an even worse conflict began in January 1854. Illinois senator Stephen A. Douglas wanted to build a railroad from Chicago to the West Coast. The land it would pass through was undeveloped. To build on that land, Congress needed to pass a law making the land a territory.

Stephen A. Douglas thought each territory should be able to decide whether to allow slavery.

Passing this law would require support from Southern lawmakers. However, the land was north of the 36°30′ parallel. Based on the Missouri Compromise, it would become a free territory. Douglas knew proslavery lawmakers would vote against it. So, he drafted a new **bill**.

The bill suggested that each territory's settlers could decide for themselves if the territory would

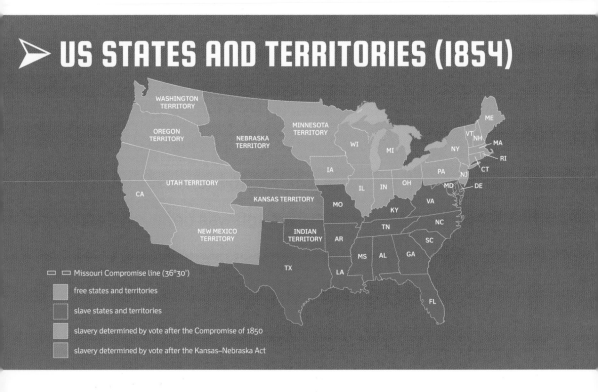

> **US STATES AND TERRITORIES (1854)**

WASHINGTON TERRITORY

OREGON TERRITORY

NEBRASKA TERRITORY

MINNESOTA TERRITORY

ME

VT
NH
MA
RI

WI

MI

NY

IA

PA

NJ
CT

UTAH TERRITORY

CA

KANSAS TERRITORY

IL
IN
OH

MO

KY

MD
DE

VA

NC

TN

NEW MEXICO TERRITORY

INDIAN TERRITORY

AR

SC

MS
AL
GA

TX

LA

FL

□ □ Missouri Compromise line (36°30′)

free states and territories

slave states and territories

slavery determined by vote after the Compromise of 1850

slavery determined by vote after the Kansas–Nebraska Act

allow slavery. The bill also divided the land into two parts. The northern part would be called Nebraska. This part was near the free state of Iowa. As a result, most settlers would likely oppose slavery. The southern part would be called Kansas. It was next to the slave state of Missouri. So, people who settled in Kansas would likely support slavery.

This plan was known as the Kansas–Nebraska Act. Antislavery lawmakers refused to support it. Even so, the bill got enough votes to become law in May 1854. Many Northerners were angry. They felt Congress had gone against the Missouri Compromise. Slavery was now free to spread anywhere in the nation.

People began settling in both new territories. In Nebraska, the process was peaceful. But in Kansas, violence broke out between the two sides.

▲ People known as Border Ruffians stirred up violence in the Kansas Territory.

Proslavery settlers rushed to the Kansas Territory. So did antislavery settlers. Fighting broke out between the two groups. People were kidnapped and killed. On May 21, 1856, proslavery forces attacked the antislavery town of Lawrence. In retaliation, abolitionist John Brown killed five proslavery men.

Soon Kansas was in turmoil. The conflict became known as Bleeding Kansas. For a while, the territory had two rival governments. One was proslavery. The other was antislavery. Federal troops came to help stop the violence, but the conflict continued for years. Eventually, Kansas became a free state. However, people on both sides remained angry.

The Kansas–Nebraska Act also prompted a new political party to form. It was called the Republican Party. Many of its leaders opposed the spread of slavery. The party ran its first candidate in the 1856 presidential election. His name was John C. Frémont. He lost to Democrat James Buchanan. But the election helped the Republicans become a major political party.

THINK ABOUT IT ◁

Lawmakers tried several compromises during the 1800s. Why do you think the peace did not last?

CHAPTER 4

MORE TROUBLES

In 1857, the debate about slavery reached the US Supreme Court. That year, the court issued its ruling on the Dred Scott case. Dred Scott had been enslaved in Missouri. He and his slaveholder went to Illinois and the Wisconsin Territory for several years. Then they returned to Missouri.

Antislavery lawyers helped Scott sue for his freedom. According to the Missouri Compromise, slavery was illegal in both Illinois and Wisconsin.

Dred Scott lived in the free state of Illinois from 1833 to 1836.

While Scott lived there, the lawyers argued, he was a free man. And once free, he should be free forever.

However, the Supreme Court ruled that the US Constitution was never intended to include black people. Neither was the Declaration of Independence. Therefore, the court claimed that the rights described in these documents did not apply to black people. They were not US citizens and had no right to sue.

Instead, the court stated that enslaved people were property. Congress could not pass a law that stopped people from taking their property into certain places. So, the court ruled, Congress did not have the power to ban slavery. The Missouri Compromise was no longer valid.

The case sparked outrage throughout the North. Many Northerners disagreed with the

A series of debates between Abraham Lincoln (standing) and Stephen A. Douglas drew large crowds.

Supreme Court's decision. They felt it forced all the states to support slavery. The decision also strengthened the Republican Party. More people joined the party and voted for its candidates. In the 1858 elections, Democrats lost 21 seats in Congress.

In Illinois, Republican Abraham Lincoln ran against Stephen A. Douglas for a seat in the US Senate. Lincoln and Douglas debated each other seven times during the **campaign.** Thousands of people across Illinois gathered to hear them.

▲ John Brown believed violence was necessary to end slavery.

Douglas won the election. But Lincoln's powerful speeches made him famous in the North. People began thinking of him as a presidential candidate for the 1860 election.

On October 16, 1859, John Brown led a raid on Harpers Ferry, Virginia. Brown had become an antislavery leader during the conflict in Kansas. Now, he intended to start a slave revolt. Along with 18 men, he attacked a federal armory. This building stored weapons. Brown planned to use them to attack slaveholders.

The raid lasted only one day. Federal troops captured Brown and his men the next morning. Even so, the attack made the South fearful. Many Southerners worried that Brown's raid would inspire others to try similar attacks.

Some people in the North expressed support for Brown. Southerners worried these people might try to invade. Thousands of Southerners joined military groups. They wanted to be prepared to fight. Many Northern citizens living in the South fled. Some were attacked or threatened. Southerners often saw them as enemies. The rift between regions had grown even deeper.

THINK ABOUT IT ◁

Brown believed only a revolt could end slavery. Do you think violence is ever the right way to make change? Why or why not?

CHAPTER 5

LEAVING THE UNION

In May 1860, the Republican Party chose Lincoln as its presidential candidate. Lincoln wanted to limit the spread of slavery. This view made him very unpopular in the South. Some states didn't even put his name on the ballot.

The Democrats had two candidates that year. Northern Democrats nominated Douglas. He wanted to let each territory decide whether to allow slavery. Southern Democrats disliked this.

A crowd gathers outside Lincoln's house during the 1860 presidential campaign.

So, they nominated John C. Breckinridge instead. He wanted to allow slavery in all territories. A third party nominated John Bell.

In October, Republicans won state elections in Pennsylvania and Indiana. That meant Lincoln would likely win the presidential election. Douglas knew how much Southern states disliked Lincoln. He worried they would secede if Lincoln won. Douglas used his own money to travel around the South and give speeches pleading for unity.

In November, Lincoln got less than 40 percent of the popular vote. And he lost in all of the slave states. Still, he won the election.

Lawmakers tried to reach another agreement in December. A few senators suggested bringing back the Missouri Compromise. New territories below the 36°30′ parallel would allow slavery. But Republicans opposed this effort. They didn't want slavery to spread at all. Southern states were also done compromising. Some believed leaving the Union was the only way to protect slavery. On December 20, 1860, South Carolina became the first state to secede. As 1861 began, six more states left the Union. They were Mississippi, Florida, Alabama, Georgia, Louisiana, and Texas.

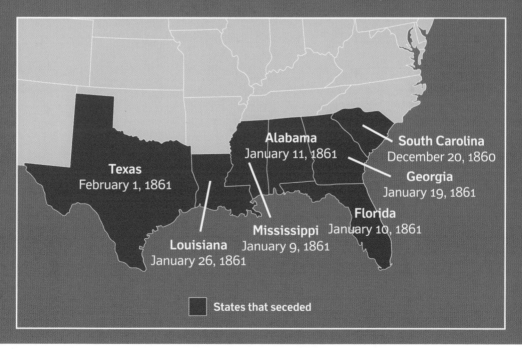

STATES BEGIN TO SECEDE ◄

Alabama
January 11, 1861

South Carolina
December 20, 1860

Georgia
January 19, 1861

Texas
February 1, 1861

Florida
January 10, 1861

Mississippi January 9, 1861

Louisiana
January 26, 1861

States that seceded

CHAPTER 6

BECOMING THE CONFEDERACY

After leaving the Union, the Southern states formed their own government. They called themselves the Confederate States of America. **Delegates** from each state met in Montgomery, Alabama, on February 4, 1861. They worked together to create a new government. Over the next six days, they drafted a temporary constitution. Then, they elected a temporary president and vice president.

Crowds of people attend the inauguration of the Confederate president on February 18, 1861.

The president and vice president would both serve for six years. They could not be reelected. Jefferson Davis became the president. His vice president was Alexander H. Stephens. Both men had previously served in the US Congress. Neither initially favored secession. In fact, Davis didn't want to be president. But he agreed to take the job. He felt he needed to be loyal to his state.

The delegates formed a temporary Congress as well. Like the US Congress, it had two bodies. One was a senate. The other was a house of representatives. Voting for permanent members of Congress was set for November. So were elections for a permanent president and vice president.

The delegates spent the next month developing a permanent constitution. It was based on the US Constitution. But there were a few key differences. The US Constitution focused on all states acting

Jefferson Davis represented Mississippi in the US Senate from 1857 to 1861.

together to achieve national goals. In contrast, the Confederate Constitution permitted each state to act independently. States could issue their own money. And they could refuse to allow the central government to use their soldiers.

The Confederate Constitution also guaranteed the right to hold slaves. It stated that the Confederate Congress would protect this right.

▲ This home in Montgomery, Alabama, served as the first White House of the Confederacy.

Congressmen could not make any laws prohibiting slavery. This rule applied to the current states and to any new territories the Confederacy might gain.

As president, Davis wanted to make sure that all states felt they were being treated equally. So, his first **cabinet** had one member from each state. The group met for the first time in a hotel room in Montgomery. This city served as the Confederacy's first capital.

In early 1861, the Confederate government was just getting started. The president's office was marked by a piece of paper stuck on the door. A visitor asked cabinet member Robert Toombs where he could find the State Department. Toombs replied that it was in his hat. He had been carrying all the State Department's important documents on his body.

At the end of February, Davis signed a law creating the Confederate States Army. It was modeled on the US Army. At the time, however, leaders didn't know how soon the army would be needed. When Davis had taken his oath of office, he said the South just wanted to be left alone.

THINK ABOUT IT ◁

Some countries have a strong central government. Others allow local governments more independence. What are some advantages and disadvantages of both systems?

CHAPTER 7

NO TURNING BACK

Lincoln took office as US president on March 4, 1861. The next day, he faced a critical decision. Fort Sumter was a federal fort in Charleston, South Carolina. The fort had not surrendered to the Confederacy when South Carolina seceded. Now, Lincoln had to decide how to respond.

Some advisors told Lincoln to hold the fort. Others told him to surrender it. To hold the fort, Lincoln would need to send food and supplies.

Lincoln wanted to bring the Confederate states back into the Union.

However, if he sent reinforcements, he risked starting a war. So, Lincoln decided to try a middle ground. He would not send more soldiers to defend the fort. But he would send food for the soldiers who were already inside.

Fort Sumter also presented a challenge for Davis. If the Confederate president allowed the fort to receive supplies, he risked appearing weak. People might accuse him of giving in to the North. However, an attack would be risky, too. The Confederacy was barely two months old. It had few ways to make weapons or supplies. And the Union states had 11 times as many ships as the states that seceded.

Davis did not want war. But he believed the Confederacy needed to control Fort Sumter. So, he decided to attack the fort before the Union ships reached it. Confederate cannons began shelling Fort Sumter in the early morning on April 12. Thirty-three hours later, the fort's defenders surrendered. The war between North and South had begun.

MORE STATES SECEDE

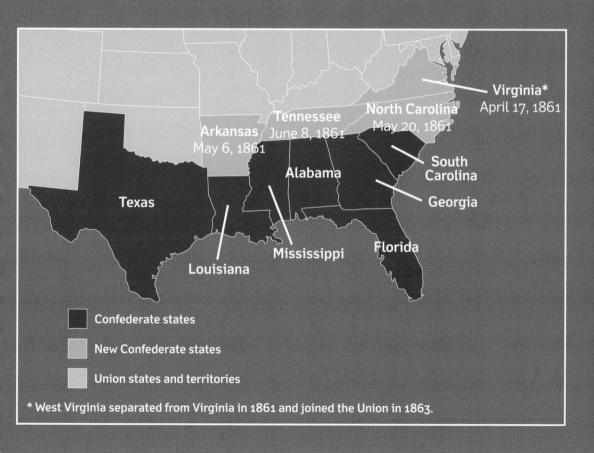

Virginia*
April 17, 1861

North Carolina
May 20, 1861

Tennessee
June 8, 1861

Arkansas
May 6, 1861

Alabama

South
Carolina

Texas

Georgia

Mississippi

Florida

Louisiana

Confederate states

New Confederate states

Union states and territories

* West Virginia separated from Virginia in 1861 and joined the Union in 1863.

The Tredegar Iron Works in Richmond, Virginia, produced most of the weapons for the Confederate army.

Lincoln called for 75,000 men to fight. In many Northern states, people rushed to enlist. However, Southerners tended to side with the Confederacy. Between April and June of 1861, four more states seceded. They were Virginia, Arkansas, North Carolina, and Tennessee.

Virginia was a key state for the Confederacy. The state had the South's largest population. Its industrial ability was almost as great as the first seven Confederate states combined. In May 1861, the Confederate government moved its capital from Montgomery to Richmond, Virginia.

When Virginia left the Union, Robert E. Lee came with it. Lee had been a member of the US military for many years. In fact, Lincoln had asked him to command the 75,000 Union troops. But Lee turned him down. A Virginia native, Lee felt he could not take part in an invasion of the South. He resigned from the US Army and joined Virginia's armed forces. Thousands of other men signed up to fight for the Confederacy. In fact, so many volunteered that 20,000 men were sent home.

For each army's leaders, there was no turning back. The United States had split apart. Both sides thought the war would last no more than three months. Neither expected the devastating battles that lay ahead.

MARY BOYKIN CHESNUT

Mary Boykin Chesnut lived in Charleston, South Carolina. Her husband owned several plantations where more than 500 enslaved people were forced to work. When South Carolina seceded, Chesnut described the split between North and South in her diary. "We are divorced because we have hated each other so," she wrote.[1]

Chesnut compared the Confederate cabinet to a loaded gun. "Dissension will break out," she wrote. "There is a perfect **magazine** of discord and discontent in that cabinet [which] only wants a hand to apply the torch."[2] Chesnut didn't think the cabinet members would work well together. And she was largely correct. Many members were chosen to make states feel equal. However, they often lacked the necessary experience or skills.

⚐ Mary Boykin Chesnut's diary is often used by people who research the Civil War.

As tension kept building, Chesnut was worried that nobody seemed concerned about the awful possibilities that war might bring. She wrote: "And so we fool on, into the black cloud ahead of us."[3]

Chesnut was lying awake in her bed in the early morning hours of April 12. She heard the first shot fired at Fort Sumter. As shells exploded, Chesnut watched and prayed.

1. Mary Boykin Chesnut. *A Diary from Dixie*. Edited by Isabella D. Martin and Myrta Lockett Avary. London: William Heinemann, 1905. 20.
2. Chesnut. *A Diary from Dixie*. 108.
3. Chesnut. *A Diary from Dixie*. 30.

FOCUS ON
THE FORMATION OF THE CONFEDERACY

Write your answers on a separate piece of paper.

1. Write a paragraph summarizing one of the political conflicts that took place in the early 1800s.

2. Do you think compromises are an effective way to resolve political conflicts? Why or why not?

3. What was the first state to secede from the Union?
   - **A.** Maryland
   - **B.** Texas
   - **C.** South Carolina

4. Why did proslavery lawmakers support the Kansas–Nebraska Act?
   - **A.** They weren't interested in slavery in newly acquired territories.
   - **B.** They hoped proslavery settlers could help Kansas become a slave state.
   - **C.** They hoped it would keep antislavery settlers away from Nebraska.

Answer key on page 48.

GLOSSARY

abolitionists
People who work to end slavery.

bill
A written plan to create or change a law.

cabinet
The group of people a president chooses to help run the government.

campaign
A series of activities such as traveling, speaking, or planning events to convince people to vote for a political candidate.

delegates
People who are selected to vote, act, or speak on behalf of others.

federal
Having to do with the top level of government, involving the whole nation rather than just one state.

fugitive
A person who is running away or hiding, often to avoid arrest or capture.

magazine
A device that holds ammunition to be fed into the chamber of a gun.

secede
To formally withdraw from a political group or nation.

tariff
A tax charged by the government on merchandise.

territories
Areas that are not states but are under government control.

TO LEARN MORE

BOOKS

Cummings, Judy Dodge. *Civil War Leaders*. Minneapolis: Abdo Publishing, 2017.

Grayson, Robert. *The U.S. Civil War: Why They Fought*. North Mankato, MN: Capstone, 2016.

Otfinoski, Steven. *The Split History of the Battle of Fort Sumter*. North Mankato, MN: Capstone, 2018.

NOTE TO EDUCATORS

Visit **www.focusreaders.com** to find lesson plans, activities, links, and other resources related to this title.

INDEX

Answer Key: 1. Answers will vary; **2.** Answers will vary; **3.** C; **4.** B